Doberman Pinschers

by Julie Murray

Abdo Kids Jumbo is an Imprint of Abdo Kids
abdobooks.com

abdobooks.com

Published by Abdo Kids, a division of ABDO, P.O. Box 398166, Minneapolis, Minnesota 55439.

Printed in the United States of America, North Mankato, Minnesota.

102025

012026

Photo Credits: Getty Images, National Archives, Shutterstock, Thinkstock

Production Contributors: Teddy Borth, Jennie Forsberg, Grace Hansen
Design Contributors: Candice Keimig, Julia Line

Library of Congress Control Number: 2025936497

Publisher's Cataloging-in-Publication Data

Names: Murray, Julie, author.

Title: Doberman Pinschers / by Julie Murray

Description: Minneapolis, Minnesota : Abdo Kids, 2026 | Series: Dogs | Includes online resources and index.

Identifiers: ISBN 9798384907510 (lib. bdg.) | ISBN 9798384908210 (ebook) | ISBN 9798384908562 (read-to-me ebook)

Subjects: LCSH: Doberman pinscher--Juvenile literature. | Watchdogs--Juvenile literature. | Working dogs--Juvenile literature. | Dogs--Juvenile literature. | Dogs--Behavior--Juvenile literature. | Animal behavior--Juvenile literature.

Classification: DDC 636.7--dc23

Table of Contents

Doberman Pinscher

Doberman pinschers are strong and smart dogs. They are also protective. This makes them good military and police dogs. They can also make great family pets!

Dobermans were first **bred** in Germany in the late 1800s. Many Dobermans served in World War I and World War II. They were messengers, **scouts**, and guard dogs.

Germany
Europe
Africa
N
W
E
S

Dobermans have a **muscular** body. They can stand 28 inches (71 cm) tall and weigh up to 100 pounds (45 kg). They are born with ears that flop forward and a long tail. Many have their ears **cropped** and tails **docked**.

Dobermans have a **sleek**, shiny coat. Their hair is short. Dobermans are often black in color, but can also be red, blue, or fawn. They have rust-colored markings.

Grooming

Dobermans need their coat brushed weekly. They also need their nails trimmed and teeth cleaned regularly.

Exercise

Dobermans are energetic dogs that need regular exercise. They love to play with toys. They enjoy a game of fetch or large areas to explore.

Dobermans are fast and can run for long periods of time. They can run up to 32 miles per hour (51.5 kph)! A daily run is a good way for them to get exercise.

Personality

Dobermans are very smart and can be trained easily. They are also **loyal** and like to stick by their owner's side. With proper training, they can be great family dogs.

Dobermans like to have a job to do. Some are guide or **therapy dogs**. Others are used in search and rescue missions.

IN TRAINING

More Facts

- Doberman pinschers are named after Karl Friedrich Louis Dobermann. He was the first person to **breed** the dog.
- Dobermans perform well in **agility**, dock diving, and flyball competitions.
- The American Kennel Club officially recognized the breed in 1908. Dobermans are members of the Working Group.

Glossary

agility – a sport where handlers guide their dogs through a timed obstacle course.

bred – developed over time for a certain purpose.

breed – a particular kind of dog.

cropped – describing dog ears that have been surgically changed to stand up straight.

docked – describing a dog tail that has been surgically shortened.

loyal – giving or showing constant support to someone or something.

muscular – having muscles that are large or strong.

scout – someone or something sent to spy or gather information.

sleek – smooth.

therapy dog – a well-trained dog that provides emotional support and comfort to people in different places, such as hospitals and schools.

Index

Visit **abdokids.com** to access crafts, games, videos, and more!

Use Abdo Kids code
DDK7510
or scan this QR code!